HIDDEN GARDENS OF BEACON HILL

Photographs by Southie Burgin

THE BEACON HILL GARDEN CLUB, INC.
Boston, Massachusetts

ACKNOWLEDGMENTS
The Editors gratefully acknowledge the advice and assistance of the
following in the preparation of this edition: David R. Godine, Frances M.
Howard, Betsy P. Leitch, Ruth C. McKay, Carolyn M. Osteen and Ropes &
Gray, Anne Swanson, J. Patrick Willoughby, Floyd Yearout, and the members
of the Beacon Hill Garden Club whose gardens appear on these pages.

THE HIDDEN GARDENS OF BEACON HILL
Published by the Beacon Hill Garden Club, Inc., 1987
Reprinted 1991

EDITORS: *Barbara W. Moore, Gail Weesner*
DESIGNER: *Dede Cummings*
TYPESETTING: *Set in Granjon by Maryland Linotype Composition*
PRINTING: *Dai Nippon, Tokyo*

Cover: A fifteenth-century miniature from a manuscript of Renaud de
Montauban; Bibliothèque Nationale, Paris. With permission.

Introduction
Beacon Hill and the Hidden Gardens

Although Beacon Hill is one of the nation's oldest urban neighborhoods, it saw no permanent development until Boston was almost two centuries old. Rough, rocky, and overgrown, the Hill was the last sizeable piece of land on Boston Neck to be developed for housing. Around 1800, however, a group of entrepreneurs known as the Mount Vernon Proprietors undertook an ambitious scheme to subdivide the Hill's south slope for "mansion houses." These custom-designed, free-standing structures were to be set on parcels of an acre or more. The scheme was short lived, and in the following decades the remainder of the Hill was built up by speculator/developers in attached row houses with minimal setback from the street.

Behind the row houses of the 1820s and 1830s were deep, narrow yards whose use was strictly functional. In those days before modern plumbing and services, the yard supported the outhouse and trash pit, as well as a variety of summer cooking and laundry activities.

Indeed, Beacon Hill entered the twentieth century with few proper gardens—only those attached to the early mansion houses. By the 1920s, however, a few homeowners had begun to turn these outdoor areas into amenities. In 1929 a small group of neighbors interested in city horticulture joined together as the Beacon Hill Garden Club. Laundry lines were removed and derelict sheds demolished; one by one, the Hidden Gardens of Beacon Hill began to flower.

Now in its fifty-eighth year, the Beacon Hill Garden Club is proud of its ever-increasing commitment to the beautification of the inner city. Proceeds from the two previous editions of this book and from the club's annual May garden tour benefit many environmental and beautification efforts. In addition to regular plantings in the Public Garden and Boston Common, the club has planned and executed streetside gardens for a number of neighborhood sites and for the Old North Church—a garden that it continues to maintain. More recently the club has contributed to the floral plantings along Storrow Drive and designed and funded new plantings at the Hatch Shell on the Charles River Esplanade. In addition, the club gives major support to such groups as the Friends of the Public Garden, the Park Ranger Program, the Massachusetts Horticultural Society, and the Arnold Arboretum.

Welcome to Beacon Hill and thank you for your interest in its hidden gardens. We hope that this little book gives you pleasure and that it may occasionally prove useful as a practical guide to the design and planting of gardens in the city.

The gardens presented in this book are unusual in one respect above all others: They are designed—and used—as extra living space, usually entered from the house by just a single step. The gardens are as much architectural as they are horticultural. Of room size—20 by 30 feet is average—each is defined by four "walls" and a "floor." Practically as well as visually, the Beacon Hill garden is an extension of the house— an extra, outdoor room.

An Outdoor Room
The Garden of Dr. and Mrs. Desmond Birkett
LOUISBURG SQUARE

t is difficult to imagine a less promising site for an outdoor room than the one occupied by this exquisite little garden. A mere 10 by 30 feet and enclosed on three sides by tall buildings, it is open only to the south, where a high brick wall faces a busy thoroughfare. When the present owners began planning the garden in 1976, it was overrun with weeds and ivy. They cleared and widened the flower beds and began experimenting with plants brought from their weekend house on Cape Cod. The garden has matured in a most enchanting way; the bed beside the house contains a well-established border of old-fashioned flowers, while the shady bed on the right supports ferns and wildflowers within a ground cover of myrtle. The rectangular concrete paving stones have acquired an interesting patina, and white azaleas and rhododendrons flank a small pool. The plants conform to the small scale of the area, and every inch of planting space has been utilized. This garden is a superb example of how a dedicated gardener has made optimal use of a small and difficult space.

An Ingenious Design
The Garden of Mr. and Mrs. Graham E. Jones
CHESTNUT STREET

Even by Beacon Hill standards, this narrow, shaded plot offered a great design challenge. The extremely high back wall, sheer and drab, presented an unfriendly face to the rear windows of the house. The most obvious remedy, letting ivies grow over the wall, would have taken several years. Instead, the owners chose an instant and more ingenious solution: they added an interesting architectural feature, an iron balcony, that breaks the vertical height of the back wall by providing a strong horizontal element. The balcony incorporates a set of three nineteenth-century medallions salvaged from a Philadelphia mansion. The balcony, the spiral staircase, and the plantings of evergreens have transformed the grim aspect of the rear wall into an attractive stage set. The only part of the garden to get much sun, the balcony displays seasonal plants—greens in winter and potted hibiscus standards during the summer months, when the urns are planted with flowering annuals.

As in most other Beacon Hill gardens, the permanent plantings include many broad-leaved evergreens. Azalea, rhododendron, holly, laurel, andromeda, pyracantha —these hardy woodland natives find the urban environment surprisingly congenial; moreover, their foliage provides an attractive backdrop of greenery year round.

A Fragrant Garden
The Garden of Mr. and Mrs. Victor Brogna
WEST CEDAR STREET

Deeply set into the slope of the hill, this garden is almost always approached—and viewed—from above, an important consideration when the owners began its rejuvenation in 1969. It was heavily shaded and entirely devoid of plant material except for the large lilac, blooming here on the left; however, it did claim a number of fine features, particularly the herringbone brick paving and a massive old granite retaining wall along the rear boundary. Another attribute was an intruder, a handsome flowering crab that branches gracefully over the south wall from the garden next door. This splendid specimen, planted by an unknown benefactor more than a century ago, is an excellent—and in this case happy—example of a "shared" tree, which, overgrowing boundary walls, becomes an important feature in a neighboring yard. This is a fragrant garden. Plants have been chosen for a succession of scents throughout the growing season. After the lilac fades, wisteria and peonies bloom. A small herb garden in a sunny corner contains some plants that are grown for culinary use and others, like lavender and santolina, grown for their fragrance alone.

A Spring Garden
The Garden of Mr. and Mrs. Richard C. Norton
OTIS PLACE

Another garden that is often viewed from above, this area was planned to screen the presence—on the other side of the grape-stake fence—of Storrow Drive, one of the busiest arteries in Boston. The primary goal has been to isolate the garden psychologically from the roar of this motor traffic. Heavily planted, this modest-sized plot supports no fewer than five trees, a dogwood, a red maple, two katsuras, and an apple. With an abundance of early-blooming seasonals and shrubs, this is definitely a spring garden. By midsummer the shrubs and trees leaf out heavily to provide a verdant screen between the house and the world beyond. The focal point of the garden is a raised bed, a technique used often on Beacon Hill. In addition to adding architectural interest, the raised bed has practical advantages. By elevating the level of the planting area, it makes gardening easier, accommodates differences in grade, and improves drainage.

A Garden with Grass
The Garden of Mr. and Mrs. Samuel Robert
MOUNT VERNON STREET

Many a Beacon Hill gardener casts an envious eye on this large and sunny space. Attached to a Victorian house of Back Bay size and scale, the garden is big enough to receive ample light and air; furthermore, it is one of the very few open spaces on Beacon Hill that boasts a lawn. The gracefully curved double stairway and balcony, which date from 1950, add a dramatic architectural element that connects the garden to the living area of the dwelling to which it belongs. The mature crabapple, whose blossoms frame this view, is probably as old as the house; the garden is large enough that this big tree is in perfect scale. Beneath the balcony is a very effective massed planting of andromeda. Elsewhere along the borders the plantings are mixed, enlivened by a variety of tones and textures. The central lawn area is encircled by a brick pathway, and the raised beds around the boundary walls accommodate the owners' collection of antique and modern sculpture.

A Long, Narrow Garden
The Garden of Mr. and Mrs. Michael K. Tooke
MOUNT VERNON STREET

Although this garden is large for Beacon Hill, it is very long and very narrow—21 by 62 feet. It has been divided into two smaller areas, each more appealing in scale and each with its particular purpose. Next to the house is the main garden, heavily shaded by two ivy-covered ailanthus trees. Its design was determined by the adults' desire for an attractive sitting area as viewed from the house. Its layout is simple with a central rectangular bed featuring a stone bird bath used as a planter. It is formal, green, and lush with broad-leaved evergreens and ivy, pleasant to view in any season. Glimpsed through the gate is the second garden—the children's play yard—with a pink azalea in glorious bloom. This area, which receives slightly more light, is planted with cheery annuals. It is large enough to accommodate a sandbox and a jungle gym, and here the children can play happily in their own domain without disturbing the tranquillity of the plants or people in the formal garden next to the house.

A Garden of Ivy
The Garden of Mrs. Taylor R. Smith
MOUNT VERNON STREET

Just next door is a garden of almost identical dimensions. It illustrates another way to deal with a too-long-and-narrow city yard. In this case the linear space has been divided subtly into three separate areas. Next to the house is a wood deck accessible from both dining room and kitchen. The deck is separated from the lower garden by a brick planter containing a hedge of yews, seen in the foreground of this picture. A short staircase leads to an area that is gently terraced and bordered with beds of staggered widths and contrasting materials—brick, field-stone, and concrete. The different levels, setbacks, and textures add interest to what might otherwise look like a brick corridor. The stone bird bath and dolphin attached to the rear wall create a focal point to punctuate the end of this long and narrow plot. Except for a dogwood and a silver maple, the garden depends primarily on English ivy, reputedly grown from a cutting taken at Canterbury Cathedral many years ago.

A Terraced Garden
The Garden of Mr. and Mrs. Stephen Mead II
WEST CEDAR STREET

This is a garden with poor light but very good "bones." The high raised terrace, constructed of Belgian block, is an interesting architectural feature that divides the area into two separate "rooms," a dining area just outside the kitchen door and a sunnier upper level for quiet sitting and more ambitious gardening. The terrace has been in place for many years, perhaps since the house was built in the 1830s. When the present owners acquired the house in 1978, they removed a large willow tree that had completely outgrown its urban setting and replaced most of the other plants as well. They have experimented with various materials while enhancing the architectural character of the garden with unusual accessories: the Chinese Chippendale-style garden bench and planter, the Victorian wrought-iron pot holder, and the stone column adapted for use as a planter. The marble container in the foreground, of unknown origin, was excavated in several pieces from beneath a flower bed; a viburnum lives happily in this planter year round. On the upper terrace grow three pygmy dogwoods and espaliered juniper, yew, and ivy. Espaliered plants are very useful features in any small garden; they provide interesting accents and maximum greenery yet occupy a minimum of ground space.

A Romantic Garden
The Garden of Dr. and Mrs. John T. Maltsberger
CHESTNUT STREET

Like any room inside the house, the outdoor room can be changed to reflect the style and taste of a new owner. Here is an example of an old garden that has been dramatically altered without undergoing any major structural change. It has, in effect, been redecorated by an imaginative and enthusiastic new owner who, by adding numerous small features, has completely transformed its atmosphere from formal and serene to eclectic and romantic. Among the most striking additions are the mirrors, a very effective garden feature. Not only do they reflect light, but they create a sense of depth and perspective and an illusion of space. The Victorian birdcage and the three-quarter-size statue of two children add other personal touches. Overlooking the garden is a greenhouse, which allows the owners to enjoy some of their garden during the long winter months.

The Connecting Gardens are a unique combination of six contiguous gardens behind Pinckney Street, West Cedar Street, and Louisburg Square. They were established in 1928 when a group of neighbors agreed to take down the barriers separating their small yards to create a larger open space. The resulting maze of low walls and hedges, pathways and steps, achieves a feeling of harmony and unity even though the gardens have always been individually owned and maintained. An overview of these gardens appears on the following page.

A Connecting Garden
The Garden of Mrs. Virginia M. Lawrence
WEST CEDAR STREET

In the smallest of the Connecting Gardens, the planting area is extremely limited. In fact, it amounts to two tiny plots, deeply shaded, that define the corner boundaries of a small paved courtyard and provide pleasant, green vignettes within the larger context of the Connecting Gardens. These pocket gardens demonstrate the use of restraint in the design of small areas. Nothing is overdone; the layout and choice of plant material are kept very simple to avoid a cluttered look. The planting in the upper photograph is a miniature woodland scene with white and red trillium and bleeding heart within a carpet of ivy. The seedling oak tree is a volunteer, planted by a squirrel returning from Boston Common, no doubt. The other area is treated more formally: A small stone squirrel, a wall basin planted with begonias, an azalea, and a rhododendron in front of a raised bed of ivy are all placed with a perfect sense of simplicity and scale.

An Eighteenth-Century Garden
The Garden of Mr. and Mrs. Walter W. Patten, Jr.

WEST CEDAR STREET

In design and in spirit, this small garden owes much to the inspiration of the eighteenth century, particularly to France and to Colonial Virginia. Its owners are inveterate travelers who enjoy collecting. In re-creating their garden they have incorporated elements of the two parts of the world they love most.

The white painted walls provide a backdrop for an extensive planting of boxwood. Four varieties grow here with only occasional winter damage, attesting to the relatively mild environment within garden walls. The Korean variety has been pruned into lollipop-style topiaries. The garden is enhanced with period accessories, while the handsome reproduction ironwork of the garden gate, circular stairway, and balcony railing are Federal in design.

The roof deck, reached either from the house or via the circular stairway, commands a sweeping view of the Connecting Gardens. Receiving more light and air than the garden, it is a pleasant place for summer entertaining. The focal point of the roof garden is an eighteenth-century lead figure of a girl holding a basket of flowers. The statue is flanked by a pair of Regency torchères.

A "Topsy" Garden
The Garden of Mrs. Charles J. Innes
PINCKNEY STREET

verlooked by a small greenhouse on the second story of the house, this informal and friendly spot is the centerpiece of the Connecting Gardens. Maintained by the same owner for almost thirty years, it is, in her words, "a 'Topsy' garden—one that just 'growed.' If a plant is happy here it stays right where it is!" Although the treatment may appear casual, this is in fact the creation of an accomplished gardener with a keen eye for design and considerable knowledge of plants. It is a garden for all seasons. The delicate, tentative greenery of early spring is accented by blossoms of forsythia, magnolia, and lilac. Several weeks later the large azalea near the kitchen door puts forth a splendid display of white blooms. Open areas among shrubs are filled with spring bulbs, followed by annuals and bedding plants that give color until the first frost. Many greenhouse plants are summered outdoors.

Towering over the Connecting Gardens and their rooftops are several ailanthus trees. A scourge to some Beacon Hill gardeners, the "tree of heaven" is actually appreciated by others. Hung with flowering plants and clad in euonymus, the tree in the foreground of this picture becomes an attractive summer garden feature.

An Informal Garden
The Garden of Mr. and Mrs. Donald J. M. Wilson
MOUNT VERNON STREET

This delightful informal garden was constructed wholly by its owners. When they acquired the property in 1968 there was no garden—only a 26-by-40-foot bare brick yard. With brave hearts and strong backs, they carried out an imaginative plan that transformed the site by opening up extensive parts of the paving for plants.

The main feature of the design is a large crescent-shaped bed, raised to the height of 18 inches. The bold, sweeping curve of the bed introduces a stunning architectural element that completely distracts the eye from the rectangular shape of the plot. Its arms encircle the sitting area, creating a snug and lovely enclosure almost completely surrounded by flowers and greenery. Three small trees serve as focal points—two spring-flowering dogwoods, seen here, and a weeping birch. Beneath the trees grow hostas and wall shrubs—mountain laurel, Japanese holly, and azalea—and ivy spills gracefully over the walls. The bed in the foreground has been planted with blooming bulbs and annuals: geraniums, primroses, purple and yellow freesia, and impatiens. Pots of fuchsia hanging from the second-story balcony provide additional color.

A Young Garden—From Scratch
The Garden of Mr. and Mrs. John X. Foley
PINCKNEY STREET

Eight years ago it would have been difficult to find a less auspicious site for a garden than this. Attached to one of the rare remaining frame houses on Beacon Hill, it had been used as a dumping ground for years. The area was surrounded by a tumbledown fence and shaded by a pair of half-dead ailanthus trees. Determining that there was nothing in the yard they wished to save, the new owners made the bold but sensible decision to start from scratch. Trees, fences, paving, and soil were all removed—by hand, via the narrow passageway that gives access to the street. By the same process new soil was hauled in, and the paved area was gently terraced with reclaimed brick to create a dining area near the kitchen door. The new fence was painted a warm silvery gray, a color that reflects light and also blends nicely with the red bricks and various shades of greenery. The plantings, begun in 1980, have prospered, and the garden has taken on an established look that completely belies its age. Even the neatly stacked wood pile becomes a picturesque feature in this delightful personal retreat, where in every corner one sees evidence of the owners' sense of optimism, imagination, and style.

Another Young Garden
The Garden of Mr. and Mrs. Richard A. Gargiulo
WEST CEDAR STREET

This thin slice of courtyard, which was also renovated in 1980, is 10 feet wide and 26 feet deep, and the new design was very thoughtfully planned to avoid a bowling-alley effect. The curved raised bed along the back wall adds height and provides a stunning focal point for the rest of the garden. It is thickly planted with yew, broad-leaved evergreens, and hosta and accentuated by a pink-flowering dogwood. The fountain features "Boy with Dolphin," a copy of a fifteenth-century work by Verrocchio. The circular pattern of the brick paving, which has the effect of stretching the width of this narrow space, is particularly effective when viewed from the upper windows of the house. The old whitewashed walls reflect a mellow light, and the pink-and-white color scheme is carried out with annuals when the spring blossoms fade.

A Nostalgic Garden
The Garden of Mr. and Mrs. Thomas C. Howard
MOUNT VERNON STREET

This dramatic view through the arch of the old service passageway reveals a glimpse of one of the oldest gardens on Beacon Hill, established more than thirty years ago and still nurtured by the same owner. It has the kind of nostalgic beauty that comes only with maturity. In this tiny space—12 by 21 feet—grow well-established borders of woodland perennials: violets, trillium, hosta, lily of the valley, bleeding heart, and Solomon's seal. The south boundary consists of a two-tiered raised bed topped by a wooden fence. This arrangement lets in light and air but still provides adequate screening, especially after the Dutchman's pipe, which climbs the fence, fills out in early summer.

The garden is rich in personal mementos. The handsome terra cotta urn and the wrought iron plant holders are souvenirs of trips abroad. The zebra panels that flank the archway were painted by the garden owner on doors inside her New York City apartment many years ago. Forced to leave the apartment when the building faced demolition, she received permission to take the doors away; they eventually arrived in Boston and have graced the entrance to this enchanting garden ever since.

The Littlest Garden
The Garden of Mr. and Mrs. A. McVoy McIntyre
PINCKNEY STREET

lthough this is one of the smallest gardens on Beacon Hill, it is also one of the most loved. Its architect-owner of thirty-five years, who is also an enthusiastic horticulturist, has lavished this tiny space with tender care, ingeniously transforming an 8-by-16-foot cul-de-sac into an intimate outdoor room that is truly an extension of the house. Because the garden receives very little direct sunlight, flowering plants are rotated between here and a south-facing solarium on the second floor of the house. The towering west wall, which robs the garden of light, is completely clad in English and Boston ivy, the latter producing clusters of autumn berries that attract flocks of local and migratory birds. The antique Victorian iron furniture, the bronze statue of a fawn, and the other decorative elements conform to the diminutive scale of the garden. The sole exception to this strict rule of scale is the mature white-blooming rhododendron in the far corner, which, it should be noted, has lived very happily for more than ten years in a pot!

A Summer Bower
The Garden of the Rt. Rev. and Mrs. John B. Coburn
CHESTNUT STREET

The twenty-year-old Concord grape arbor spanning the width of this garden creates a cool and secluded summer bower. The trellis structure, by providing a roof to the enclosure, adds to the feeling of an outdoor room. In summer a thick growth of vines forms a shady retreat from the midday sun, which can be intense within brick garden walls; in winter the vines shed their leaves and the "roof" opens to let in precious light and sun. The paving is composed of concrete stones and basket-weave squares of old Beacon Hill brick laid in a bold harlequin design. Plants, many of them espaliered, are confined to narrow beds around the boundary walls, providing plenty of room for entertaining around the stone shell fountain in the center of the garden. Despite somewhat limited light, the grape arbor produces an ample harvest. Several large baskets of fruit are gathered each year and processed for jellies and wines.

An Old-World Garden
The Garden of Mrs. Charles Townsend
CHESTNUT STREET

xpertly planned and beautifully matured, this is to many minds the show-piece of Beacon Hill gardens. Elegant and serene, it possesses an ethereal beauty and old-world charm that is a tribute to its owner of almost fifty years and an inspiration to city gardeners everywhere.

A Rock Garden
The Garden of Mr. and Mrs. Thomas E. Weesner
PINCKNEY STREET

Until recently this garden was heavily shaded by a century-old American elm, which became diseased in the mid-1970s and was most reluctantly taken down. While the loss of the elm dramatically improved the horticultural potential of this southward-facing site, the root system still occupied a considerable portion of the yard. Removing it would have involved major excavation perilously close to the foundations of existing buildings and walls. The problem was solved by treating the area as a raised bed and establishing a rock garden. The unusable portions of the bed were laid over with rocks and the intervening planting pockets filled with a combination of alpines, wildflowers, and annuals. The scheme has offered the opportunity for great variety and experimentation. Among the plants that do well here are various ferns and sedums, lamium, woodland phlox, candytuft, creeping speedwell, and sweet woodruff.

A Trim and Tidy Garden
The Garden of Mr. and Mrs. Richmond Mayo-Smith
MOUNT VERNON STREET

This site once consisted of a solid concrete slab that served as a parking lot. When the new owners created a garden in 1976, they very practically decided to save room for parking, and the garden was designed accordingly. A lower area adjacent to the house is roofed with an overhead trellis. Mature wisteria climbs the trellis, filling out beautifully by midsummer and providing cool shade for summer dining. The parking area is surfaced with crushed stone and features a central decorative medallion in brick, inspired by the Boston Massacre Memorial. When the automobile is not present, this feature can be topped with an abstract terra cotta sculpture, as shown here, cleverly disguising a drain cover. The garden is trim and tidy; well-planned beds, slightly raised and set in gentle curves, support a variety of wall shrubs. Seen here are boxwood, flowering quince, espaliered yew, azalea, laurel, and dwarf varieties of two old-fashioned favorites, lilac and forsythia.

One of the most prolific builders in the early nineteenth century was Cornelius Coolidge, and among Coolidge's most ambitious projects was an entire block of houses on West Cedar Street. Built on speculation, the block was divided into parcels of almost the same size, on which almost identical houses were built. A century and a half of separate histories has individualized the houses inside and out. The following pages show four gardens in this row—all the same age, all with the same western exposure and limited sun, all of the same dimension (19 by 30 feet). Because of the personal tastes and needs of their owners (or of a succession of owners), these plots have evolved into gardens of great individuality in both ambiance and design.

A Green-and-White Garden
The Garden of Mr. and Mrs. Richard L. Brickley
WEST CEDAR STREET

Designed in 1979, this is a green-and-white garden, planned to assure a succession of white blossoms throughout the growing season and plenty of greenery year round. Spring is announced by the blooming of trillium, followed by white azaleas and rhododendrons and spring-flowering dogwood. The clematis and summer-flowering dogwood bloom through midsummer, when white impatiens and potted geraniums are set out, to be replaced by white chrysanthemums in the fall.

The herringbone brick pattern gives a lovely sense of texture to the central paved area, which is surrounded by low beds, curved at the corners to soften the squared-off angles of the outer walls. A tall lattice fence extends the height of the back wall, and a figure of Pan pipes water into a small pool.

A Formal Garden
The Garden of Mr. and Mrs. Winthrop G. Minot
WEST CEDAR STREET

The basic layout of this family garden is architectural and formal with grace-fully curving raised serpentine beds that give a sense of symmetry. Completed in 1981, it has both a sunny and a shady side, so the challenge has been to reinforce the apparent symmetry with plant material that can survive in both locations. American holly, ferns, hosta, and azalea have been particularly successful in this respect. The sunny side is shown here, with a white-flowering dogwood and interesting *trompe l'oeil* trelliswork that supports espaliered pyracantha. The paving is granite and bluestone, and the fountain features a small statue of a satyr, the work of the nineteenth-century American sculptor Albert Atkins. The owner of this garden is most enthusiastic about the raised beds: "Not only do they bring the plant material to eye level, but they're functional—a comfortable height for sitting." In addition, she notes, this arrangement is ideal for a family with a dog and small children. "Plants are raised up to a safe height, so nothing can be damaged."

A Well-Furnished Room
The Garden of Dr. and Mrs. Robert K. Hillier
WEST CEDAR STREET

With its fine sense of color and its attention to detail, it is no surprise to learn that this is the garden of an interior designer. The garden was already mature when the family moved into the house in 1980. With a discerning eye, the new owner chose to retain its most attractive features: the established beds of English ivy, the fine old hydrangea twining its way up a tall ailanthus tree, and the treatment of the rear wall with redwood window boxes below a picket fence. The fountain sculpture of two small boys standing on a shell is by Anne Kopper. Because this is a shady site, the original garden was mostly green. To introduce more color, the new owner turned to the things she knew best—furniture and accessories. The distinctive French wire furniture was discovered in an antique shop in Maine: "What I like about these pieces is their lacy, airy quality. They are a bit whimsical, but formal as well, and on a sunny day they cast beautiful shadows on the bricks." Fitted with pink cushions of floral chintz, the ensemble gives this lovely old garden the aspect of a well-furnished room.

A Green Room
The Garden of Mrs. Earl H. Eacker
WEST CEDAR STREET

 view through the arched service entrance shows how perfectly this house has been related to its garden. The back wall of the house has been given the careful treatment usually reserved for the facade, so that the house and garden flow together as if designed as a unit. The house becomes, in effect, a facade or a backdrop against which the garden is displayed, and the garden becomes in every way a natural extension of the house, a restful and relaxing green room.

The garden has been terraced to provide a sitting area next to the house. On the lower level the planting is extremely simple, depending mostly on elegant side beds of thirty-year-old mountain laurel. A native woodland plant, the laurel has grown tall and wide, obviously responding to the extra warmth and protection provided by the garden walls. In fact, woodland plants as a group do very well in city gardens, where growing conditions are not unlike those of the forest—deep shade, acid soil, poor air circulation, and a moist atmosphere.

A Family Garden

Here is another superb example of the garden as outdoor room. Entered from either the dining room or the kitchen, it serves as an extension of both areas as well as a play yard for two young children. Along the kitchen wing, a Concord grape vine cascades from the roof deck above, and English ivy and hydrangea climb from a curved bed below. A pair of old ailanthus trees rise from the narrow bed on the left; in this yard the "tree of heaven" adds a sense of scale to the enclosure and becomes a prominent, even elegant, garden feature. A young golden chain tree occupies the far corner, while other plantings along the boundary walls include American holly, rhododendron, mountain laurel, and arborvitae. All the beds are slightly raised and set in gentle free-form curves, which please the eye while softening the rectangular outline of this cheerful family garden.

A Roof Garden
The Garden of Mr. and Mrs. Garret Schenck
WEST CEDAR STREET

Sometime during the late nineteenth century, a large two-story extension was added to this house. The extension greatly increased the size of the house but reduced the garden area to a dark and narrow passageway. When the present owners bought the house in 1974, they quickly decided that the sensible place for a garden would be the roof of the ell, which offered more space and more favorable growing conditions than the tiny courtyard below. The decision required major construction. Rotted wooden decking was removed from the roof, which was then paved with old bricks.

The greatest challenge of designing the garden was providing some privacy from the dozens of windows overlooking the rooftop. The solution was a five-foot-high enclosure of lattice fencing, topped with planting boxes in strategic locations. The fence defines the boundaries of the garden; the lattice construction serves as a visual screen and gives some protection from sun and wind, yet lets in air and light.

The amount of plant material in this garden is surprising. More than seventy chrysanthemums were set out in boxes at the time of this photograph! All the plant material is confined to containers. The owner, who is an interior designer, believes that container gardening offers distinct advantages in any small, confined space: "Plants can be replaced or rearranged to create different effects at different times of the year. They can be used to camouflage unattractive features like downspouts and drains. Grouped together, they can provide wonderful shows of color and greenery and yet are easy to maintain."

A Decorous Garden
The Garden of Dr. and Mrs. Donald R. Korb
BRIMMER STREET

The basic design of this garden is a clever reversal of the usual plan for city plots—that is, to place the sitting area outside the back door and to concentrate plants toward the rear of the site. To reach the paved sitting area of this garden, one must walk from the house down a flagstone path that curves gently through a miniature woodland landscape. The pathway is flanked with hostas. On one side are massed plantings of andromeda and rhododendron; on the other side is a bed of river stones, planted with laurel, azaleas, and a hemlock tree growing straight and tall. Emerging from the woodland path, one enters an entirely different garden. The design of the sitting area is formal and restrained. Parallel flower beds are planted for seasonal color. Brickwork and fencing are tidy and trim. A silverbell tree and two flowering cherries provide a canopy of dappled shade, and the white-painted Victorian furniture adds a note of decorum.

An Outdoor Study
The Garden of Mr. and Mrs. Henry Lee
MOUNT VERNON STREET

This all-green garden has the pleasing atmosphere of an outdoor study. The long, narrow site has been divided into two separate areas. For years the owners struggled with the difficulties of dense shade and poor air circulation; the list of failures would have discouraged any but the most determined gardener. The ultimate solution was also the most practical: to invest in the tried-and-true and to create an all-green garden with hardy plant material. This photograph shows that such treatment need not be dull. By varying the shades of green and the size, texture, and shape of plants, it is possible to create an attractive and interesting effect. The bold foliage of hosta stands in fine relief against the ground cover of English ivy, and the delicately textured Japanese hollies give height to the plantings. A well-planned green garden does not require much added color. A single hanging pot of impatiens provides a focal point for the prevailing theme of pleasant greenery.

An Enchanted Garden
The Garden of Mr. and Mrs. Peter Hopkinson
WEST CEDAR STREET

The air of enchantment that lingers about this place creates the impression of an older garden. In fact, it is less than a year old and until very recently was a play yard. Its stunning transformation, accomplished during a single growing season, is the result of rather thoughtful long-range planning.

When the family moved into the house in 1973, the terraced garden had been neglected. They decided to concentrate their initial gardening efforts on the lower level and to turn over the upper terrace to the children. Here the floor was laid with wood chips, and a large jungle gym was installed. However, anticipating the day when the children would be grown, the owners saved some of the more interesting plants: the honey locust in the far corner of the yard, the rose growing on the side-wall trellis, an old and twisted wisteria vine, and a large yew, which they began to train in the manner of a bonsai. In addition, they established tentative planting beds around the boundary walls, investing only in ground-cover plants and hardy perennials that could withstand occasional abuse.

Consequently, when the play-yard era came to an end, several permanent features were already in place. The owners had only to replace the wood chips with brick paving, extend the boundary planting, and install the fountain and other accessories that they had gradually collected through the years. The result was an "instant" garden so cleverly designed that each corner presents a happy view.

A Hanging Garden
The Garden of Lise and Myles D. Striar
PINCKNEY STREET

A mere 15 by 30 feet, this garden is a stunning example of how climbers can provide lushness, privacy, and the illusion of space in a small city yard. Growing vertically, climbing plants reward the gardener with much more greenery for the ground space they occupy than any other kind of plant. Here they also soften a somewhat formal plan, making the garden seem remote and secret.

The walls have been completely clad with a quartet of mature climbers that do well in the city, adding seasonal interest from spring to fall. In May wisteria, which has ascended the entire height of a tall ailanthus tree, presents a 40-foot curtain of lavender blooms; in June come the crisp white blossoms of the climbing hydrangea; by midsummer the Dutchman's pipe is full and lovely; finally, the China fleece-vine, which grows on a trellis upon the rear wall, produces flowers in late summer and fall. Needless to say, this glorious profusion did not just happen; the garden is about thirty years old. The "vertical" garden provides a permanent backdrop for seasonal plantings—spring bulbs, summer annuals, and autumn chrysanthemums. In late fall the climbers shed their leaves, revealing the formal "bones" of the winter garden.

A Summer Garden
The Garden of Mr. and Mrs. Robert L. Fondren
JOY STREET

nlike most Beacon Hill gardens, which are planned to look their best in spring, this one does not reach its prime until midsummer when the climbers are in full leaf and the roses bloom. This garden is ideal for a family whose work schedules dictate that they spend most of the summer in town.

The slope of the hill divides the site into two levels. The lower level, nearest the house, is used for outdoor sitting and dining. The upper level, shown here, is almost square with wide, slightly raised planting beds along the boundary walls. Each bed has a somewhat different exposure, and each has been planted accordingly. The area to the right is rather shady; it contains informal woodland plants and wildflowers. The opposite bed receives enough sun to support roses; a pink standard and a white climber do very well here. Along the rear wall conditions are ideal for climbers— shady at ground level and sunny above—and the treatment of this area shows how useful climbers can be for screening out unwanted views. Directly behind a portion of the back wall is a roof deck that threatened the privacy of this family retreat. Here the wall has been heightened with a span of fencing, and three climbing plants —ivy, hydrangea, and clematis—have been allowed to intermingle, weaving through the wooden slats to form a thick green curtain of privacy between the garden and the offending roof deck.

A Practical Garden
The Garden of Mr. and Mrs. Frederic C. Church, Jr.
CHESTNUT STREET

An elegant, formal planting provides the focal point in a garden whose primary use is strictly practical—it doubles as an open-air garage. On Beacon Hill this is a rare and coveted amenity, but the decision to create the garage greatly reduced the usable gardening area and this space had to be very well planned. The beds, raised to a height of 24 inches, were designed with great formality and restraint. The espaliered pyracantha, only four years old, demonstrates how well this handsome and hardy plant does in the city. It sends forth delicate white blossoms in spring and clusters of orange berries in the fall. Other permanent plantings are also evergreen—box, rhododendron, and yew. The remainder of the bed is reserved for free-blooming annuals, allowing the gardener to change her decorative scheme from season to season or from year to year. This is a very practical garden requiring little maintenance.

An L-Shaped Garden
The Garden of Dr. and Mrs. J. Wallace McMeel
WEST CEDAR STREET

The shape of this garden is quite common on Beacon Hill, where many houses have received later additions. The L-shaped remnant of the original yard wraps around the "ell" of the house, creating a narrow enclosure on two axes. In this garden the longer axis was a cheerless corridor, about eight feet wide, beginning at the rear gate and dead-ending at the main part of the house. Because this part of the garden was most visible from indoors, the owners wanted it to be as attractive as possible. Along the boundary wall they planted a broad border of shade-tolerant shrubs and ground cover. To connect the garden to the house, they built a small raised deck, which serves as a pleasant sitting area for family use. The deck is well appointed, with handsome cast-iron furniture of Italianate design. An unusual eighteenth-century kitchen pot rack fits neatly into one corner, screening the lower part of an electric cable that runs up the rear wall of the house. Bright red flowers create a dramatic effect, viewed from either indoors or out.

A Large and Airy Garden
The Garden of Mr. and Mrs. Leonard J. Saulnier
PINCKNEY STREET

Laid out on three levels, this large garden is filled with an abundant variety of trees, shrubs, and vines, indicating the number of plants that, given sufficient light and air, can survive and even thrive in the city. Two Sargent cherry trees, a hawthorn, a golden chain, a corkscrew willow, and a flowering crabapple tree shade the garden. Honeysuckle, bittersweet, akebia, clematis, China fleecevine, and ivy scramble over walls and trellises. Winged euonymus, cotoneaster, flowering quince, privet, yew, and holly lend height to the outer beds, while a host of perennials, bulbs, and wildflowers grow everywhere within the lush ground cover of ivy and pachysandra.

When the present owners bought this house in 1965, they inherited an already mature garden, which they have appreciated and nurtured. They have retained the basic plan and major features, such as the *trompe l'oeil* mural in a recessed arch on the rear wall and the ornamental ironwork between brick piers—originally a section of balcony attached to the front of this house. Replacing plant material as necessary, they have added many personal touches, most notably the recirculating fountain, crafted from rocks found on the site, statuary, and other decorative elements.

A Country Garden
The Garden of Mr. and Mrs. Roger Allan Moore
WEST CEDAR STREET

The clothesline hooks that now support hanging pots recall an era when this was a drying yard. Today it is a working garden whose owner enjoys introducing new plant material each year. Occasionally frustrated by the confines of her city plot, she admits to an occasional yearning for the country setting of her childhood. Perhaps it is not surprising, then, that one finds here the undeniable spirit of a country garden. The borders are filled with old-fashioned flowers—columbine, coral bells, bleeding heart, violets, iris—whose continuing bloom makes this city garden as colorful as one in the country. Clematis and trumpet vine grow against the wooden siding of the original shed, and the kitchen window box supports a small but vigorous collection of herbs. House plants, which benefit from summering outdoors, are massed below the window and camouflage the cellar hatchway, an unattractive but necessary feature of most city yards.

An Eclectic Garden
The Garden of Mrs. Philip Bourne
MOUNT VERNON STREET

The engaging eccentricity of this happy little yard echoes the eclectic spirit of the house itself—a bright yellow half-timbered 1860 cottage that Oliver Wendell Holmes dubbed "Castle Sunflower." The garden was created about sixty years ago by Mrs. Frank A. Bourne, the founder and first president of the Beacon Hill Garden Club. It was Mrs. Bourne who, in 1929, began encouraging her neighbors to turn their own neglected drying yards into gardens—a trend that has continued ever since. This garden is quite different from the red-brick courtyards seen elsewhere on Beacon Hill. Indeed, part of its charm derives from the cheerful abandon with which building materials are combined. Brick, flagstone, stucco, wood, terra cotta, cement, and ironwork are assembled in a pleasant jumble of angles, textures, and forms. The telltale break in the brickwork on the rear wall marks the height of the original garden wall, a reminder that in its early years this garden was a much sunnier spot.

A Fine Old Garden
The Garden of Misses Natalie and Pauline Hébert
WEST CEDAR STREET

This fine old garden is so well established that it practically cares for itself. The flowering crabapple tree, the beds of English ivy, and the vigorous stands of Solomon's seal have been in place for thirty-five years; except for the setting out of annuals and a yearly pruning, the yard needs little maintenance. Formal in style, it is built on three levels. Each level is defined by a pair of ornamental fruit baskets; these and other garden accessories of aged terra cotta blend beautifully with the red brick walls and pavement. The ivy ground cover has been trained to climb the walls on wire leaders, creating delicate patterns of greenery; it is not, however, permitted to grow rampant. Bright blue-green shutters add color and charm to one of the oldest and most delightful gardens on Beacon Hill.

Plant List

The following is a listing of plant material that can be found in Beacon Hill gardens. The common name appears in the left-hand column, the botanical name on the right. If a particular species is known to do especially well, it is named; if only the genus is named, more than one species has been grown successfully.

✑ TREES

APPLE or CRABAPPLE	*Malus*
CHERRY	*Prunus*
CORKSCREW WILLOW	*Salix matsudana 'Tortuosa'*
DOGWOOD	*Cornus*
EUROPEAN MOUNTAIN ASH	*Sorbus aucuparia*
GOLDEN CHAIN TREE	*Laburnum anagyroides*
HEMLOCK	*Tsuga*
HONEY LOCUST	*Gleditsia*
KATSURA	*Cercidiphyllum japonicum*
MAGNOLIA	*Magnolia*
MAPLE	*Acer*
PEAR	*Pyrus*
SILVERBELL	*Halesia carolina*
TREE OF HEAVEN	*Ailanthus altissima*
WEEPING BIRCH	*Betula pendula*

✑ SHRUBS

ANDROMEDA	*Pieris*
AZALEA	*Rhododendron*
BITTERSWEET	*Celastrus orbiculatus*
BOXWOOD	*Buxus*
BRIDAL WREATH	*Spiraea*
COTONEASTER	*Cotoneaster*
ENKIANTHUS	*Enkianthus campanulatus*
EUONYMUS	*Euonymus*
FIRE THORN	*Pyracantha coccinea*
FLOWERING QUINCE	*Chaenomeles*
FORSYTHIA	*Forsythia*
HOLLY	*Ilex*
JUNIPER	*Juniperus*
LAUREL	*Kalmia*

LEUCOTHOE	*Leucothoe*
LILAC	*Syringa*
MOCK ORANGE	*Philadelphus*
PRIVET	*Ligustrum*
RHODODENDRON	*Rhododendron*
SLENDER DEUTZIA	*Deutzia gracilis*
SWEET SHRUB	*Calycanthus floridus*
VIBURNUM	*Viburnum*
YEW	*Taxus*

VINES

AKEBIA	*Akebia quinata*
BOSTON IVY	*Parthenocissus tricuspidata*
CHINA FLEECE-VINE or SILVER LACE VINE	*Polygonum aubertii*
CLEMATIS	*Clematis*
CLIMBING HYDRANGEA	*Hydrangea petiolaris*
DUTCHMAN'S PIPE	*Aristolochia durior*
ENGLISH IVY	*Hedera helix*
HONEYSUCKLE	*Lonicera japonica*
ROSE	*Rosa*
TRUMPET VINE	*Campsis radicans*
VIRGINA CREEPER or WOODBINE	*Parthenocissus quinquefolia*
WISTERIA	*Wisteria*

PERENNIALS

BELLFLOWER	*Campanula*
BLEEDING HEART	*Dicentra spectabilis*
CANDYTUFT	*Iberis sempervirens*
CHRYSANTHEMUM	*Chrysanthemum*
COLUMBINE	*Aquilegia*
CORALBELLS	*Heuchera sanguinea*
DEAD NETTLE	*Lamium*
DUTCHMAN'S BREECHES	*Dicentra cucullaria*
LILY	*Lilium*
LILY OF THE VALLEY	*Convallaria majalis*
LUNGWORT	*Pulmonaria*
PEONY	*Paeonia*
PRIMROSE	*Primula*

ROCK CRESS	*Arabis*
ROSE	*Rosa*
SPEEDWELL or VERONICA	*Veronica*
VIOLET	*Viola*
WORMWOOD	*Artemesia*

✿ GROUND COVER

BUGLEWEED	*Ajuga reptans*
HEN AND CHICKENS	*Sempervivum tectorum*
MYRTLE or PERIWINKLE	*Vinca minor*
PACHYSANDRA	*Pachysandra terminalis*
PLANTAIN LILY	*Hosta*
STONECROP	*Sedum*
SWEET WOODRUFF	*Galium odoratum*
WILD GINGER	*Asarum*

✿ BULBS

CROCUS	*Crocus*
DAFFODIL	*Narcissus*
GRAPE HYACINTH	*Muscari*
IRIS	*Iris*
ORNAMENTAL ONION	*Allium*
SCILLA	*Scilla*
SNOWDROP	*Galanthus*
STAR OF BETHLEHEM	*Ornithogalum umbellatum*
TULIP	*Tulipa*
WINTER ACONITE	*Eranthis*

✿ WILDFLOWERS

FALSE SOLOMON'S SEAL	*Smilacina*
FERNS	
JACK IN THE PULPIT	*Arisaema triphyllum*
LADY'S SLIPPER	*Cypripedium*
MOSS PINK	*Phlox subulata*
PARTRIDGEBERRY	*Mitchella repens*
SOLOMON'S SEAL	*Polygonatum biflorum*
TRILLIUM	*Trillium*
VIOLET	*Viola*
WILD GERANIUM	*Geranium maculatum*